Baby Animals

Five Stories of Endangered Species

For Spencer and Serena
D. H.

For Joanna and Lucy
J. B.

Baby Animals

Five Stories of Endangered Species

by Derek Hall
illustrated by John Butler

WALKER BOOKS

AND SUBSIDIARIES

LONDON • BOSTON • SYDNEY

First published individually as
Panda Climbs (1984), *Tiger Runs* (1984), *Elephant Bathes* (1985),
Polar Bear Leaps (1985), *Gorilla Builds* (1985) by
Walker Books Ltd, 87 Vauxhall Walk, London SE11 5HJ
Collected edition published 1993

This edition published 1995

2 4 6 8 10 9 7 5 3

Text © 1984, 1985, 1988, 1989 Derek Hall
Illustrations © 1984, 1985, 1992 John Butler

This book has been typeset in Veronan Light Educational.

Printed in Hong Kong

British Library Cataloguing in Publication Data
A catalogue record for this book is
available from the British Library.

ISBN 0-7445-3030-X

Contents

Balega the Elephant
11
Khana the Tiger
21
Chi-li the Panda
31
Laska the Polar Bear
41
Simbi the Gorilla
51
Natural history notes
60

Balega
the Elephant

Balega is playing while his mother munches
leaves. He runs around shaking his head
and waggling his ears.

What's that? Balega sees something moving in an old tree. He carefully stretches out his trunk and puts the tip inside a hole.

Ouch! Balega jumps back. Something has
stung him and it hurts. Suddenly, hornets
come flying out, buzzing
around him angrily.

Balega runs back to his mother, squealing.
He is frightened. She gently strokes his
face with her trunk to make him
feel better.

Balega and his mother go down to the pool.
They both drink, sucking up water in their
trunks and squirting it down their throats.

Balega's mother rolls over on her side.
Balega tries to climb on top of her but keeps
slipping and sliding off. It's great fun.

They have a lovely time splashing and swishing about with their trunks. Then Balega squirts water over his mother. She likes it, too!

After their bath, they blow dust over themselves.
It sticks to their wet skins and keeps them cool.
Best of all, it stops insects biting!

Khana
the Tiger

Khana is feeling so bored. Her mother has gone hunting for food. Hunting is very dangerous, so Khana must stay in a safe place.

Khana wants to play. What's that? Something
is moving in the grass. She trots over to see.
It's a beautiful butterfly.

Khana tries to touch the butterfly, but it darts
away. She scampers after it.
Again and again she tries
to catch it with her paw.

Khana is lost! She has chased the
butterfly for such a long way.
And now it is raining. She sits
down and cries like a kitten.

Suddenly, there's a noise! Khana looks up,
frightened. A huge elephant is lumbering
towards her. It's the biggest animal she
has ever seen.

Khana turns and runs, faster than she has
ever run before. She is running like the
wind, and crying
for her mother.

Khana hears her mother's roar, and runs to meet
her. Khana's mother is very cross. But Khana is
so pleased to see her again.

Khana's mother soon forgives her. They lie
down, and Khana climbs on to her. She purrs
happily, feeling safe once more.

Chi-li
the Panda

Chi-li loves to play with his mother. Sometimes
she gives him a piggy-back and then he
feels as tall as a grown-up panda.

Soon, it is dinnertime. The grown-ups eat lots of
bamboo shoots, crunching the juicy stems.
Chi-li likes to chew the soft leaves.

The grown-ups eat for such a long time, they always fall asleep afterwards. Chi-li scampers off to play. He rolls over and over in the snow and tumbles down a hill.

When Chi-li stops at the bottom
he cannot see his mother any more.
But he sees a leopard! Chi-li is
very frightened.

He scrambles over to the nearest tree and
climbs up. Chi-li has never climbed before,
and it is so easy! He digs his claws into
the bark and goes up and up.

Soon, he is near the top. Chi-li feels so good
up here. And he can see such a long way over
the mountains and trees and snow of China.

Chi-li hears his mother crying. She is looking for him. He starts to climb down. But going down is harder than climbing up, and he slips. Plop! He lands in the snow.

Chi-li's mother is so happy. She gathers
him up in her big furry arms and cuddles
him. It is lovely to be warm and safe
with her again.

Laska
the Polar Bear

Laska the polar bear is big enough to leave
the den where he was born. For the first time
he plays outside in the soft snow.

Soon, it is time to go to the sea for food. Laska's
mother is hungry. He rides high on her back,
gripping her fur with excitement.

While his mother is busy eating, Laska wanders off. He stands up on his hind legs, as tall as he can, to look out over the Arctic Sea.

Suddenly, the ice breaks! A small ice-floe carries
Laska away from the land, and he is too young
to swim! He whimpers for his mother.

She roars to her cub in alarm. Bravely he
leaps across the gap towards her.
It is almost too far! His paws
slither on the icy shore.

Just in time his mother grasps him by the
neck. She hauls him, dripping wet, from
the water. Laska hangs limp and miserable
from her strong jaws.

On firm land again, he shakes himself like
a dog to dry his fur. His mother wants
to find a safe place to sleep. Laska
follows her like a shadow.

Now Laska is hungry. His mother feeds him
with her milk. Then he snuggles up to her
warm body and goes to sleep.

Simbi
the Gorilla

Simbi and her father finish their dinner in the
forest. She has eaten lots of tasty leaves.
He likes to chew on juicy stalks as well.

Simbi's father is sleepy and decides to make a
nest. He bends stalks and leaves over and treads
on them until they are soft. Simbi watches.

Her father settles back on the nest, wriggling around and stretching until he is comfortable. Poor Simbi – there's no room for her!

Simbi wants to make her own nest. She climbs
a tree near her father and rocks backwards
and forwards on it. It's fun – it's like a swing.

But Simbi is a bit too heavy. And the tree is a
bit too thin. It suddenly bends right over
and Simbi slips. She is falling...

She lands on top of her father and wakes
him up. He scrambles to his feet, grumpy
and grumbling. Simbi hurries away.

Simbi climbs a stronger tree. She bends leafy
twigs and branches over. Then she tramples
on them to make a soft cushion of leaves.

Simbi has done it – made her first nest high up in a tree! She snuggles down and nibbles some more leaves. Simbi feels just like a grown-up.

Natural history notes

Elephants like Balega live in Africa. Mother elephants and their families travel around in groups called herds. Most of the grown-up members of the herd are sisters. Elephants have only one baby at a time, so Balega probably plays with cousins his own age, not with his older brothers and sisters. A little elephant will stay with his mother's herd for twelve years or more; by then he will be nearly grown up.

Tigers like Khana live in India and nearby hot countries, though a few are found in cold northern forests. A mother tiger usually has a family of three or four cubs – sometimes as many as six. She feeds them on milk for several months, then helps them learn how to hunt other animals. Khana and her brothers and sisters will stay with their mother until they are nearly three years old. By this time they will be good hunters, and able to fend for themselves.

Giant pandas like Chi-li live on the slopes of high mountains in China. They are among the rarest animals in the world, and because of this they have become the symbol for the World Wide Fund for Nature. Mother pandas usually have one baby at a time and care for it for about six months. Then the young panda leaves to search for food on its own. The panda has a special extra thumb on each of its front feet, which helps it to hold the bamboo shoots that it eats.

Polar bears like Laska live near the sea in the far north of the world. At the beginning of the winter, the mother polar bear digs a deep den in the snow. Her three or four babies, who are the size of guinea pigs, are born there at about Christmas time. They stay warmly cuddled up to her and feed on her milk for about three months – then they are big enough to venture out of the den. Polar bears stay with their mothers for two to three years. By then they are large and can hunt for themselves.

Simbi and her father, like all other wild gorillas, live in Africa. Though they are large, gorillas are peaceable animals. Family groups travel around a home area in forests near the equator, looking for the plants they like to eat. They also spend a good deal of time resting. All gorillas can climb quite well, but the big males, like Simbi's father, usually make comfortable beds on the ground. Baby gorillas generally sleep beside their mothers until they are about two years old, but they do practise making nests for themselves. Simbi's playmates are probably her cousins, for her mother is not likely to have another baby until Simbi is about four years old.